Harold Pinter was born in London in 1930. He is married to Antonia Fraser. In 1995 he was awarded the David Cohen British Literature Prize, for a lifetime's achievement in literature. In 1996 he was given the Laurence Olivier Award for a lifetime's achievement in theatre.

Works by Harold Pinter published by Grove Press

Complete Works: One (The Birthday Party • The Room • The Dumb Waiter • A Slight Ache • A Night Out • "The Black and White" • "The Examination" • "Writing for the Theatre")

Complete Works: Two (The Caretaker • The Dwarfs [play] • *The Collection • The Lover • Night School • Trouble in the Works • The Black and White • Request Stop • Last to Go • Special Offer •* "Writing for Myself")

Complete Works: Three (The Homecoming • The Basement • Landscape • Silence • Night • That's Your Trouble • That's All • Applicant • Interview • Dialogue for Three • Tea Party [play] • "Tea Party" [short story] • "Mac")

Complete Works: Four (Old Times • No Man's Land • Betrayal • Monologue • Family Voices)

PLAYS AND SCREENPLAYS

Ashes to Ashes
Betrayal
The Birthday Party and The Room
The Caretaker and The Dumb Waiter
Five Screenplays (The Servant • The Pumpkin Eater • The Quiller Memorandum • Accident • The Go-Between)
The Homecoming
Moonlight
Mountain Language
No Man's Land
Old Times
One for the Road
Other Places: Three Plays (A Kind of Alaska • Victoria Station • Family Voices)
Party Time and The New World Order

POETRY AND PROSE

Collected Poems and Prose
The Dwarfs: A Novel
100 Poems by 100 Poets (an anthology selected by Harold Pinter, Geoffrey Godbert, and Anthony Astbury)
99 Poems in Translation (an anthology selected by Harold Pinter, Geoffrey Godbert, and Anthony Astbury)

HAROLD PINTER

Ashes to Ashes

Grove Press
New York

First published in Great Britain in 1996 by Faber and Faber Limited
First Grove Press edition, April 1997

Printed in the United States of America

Library of Congress Cataloging-in-Publication Data
Pinter, Harold, 1930–
Ashes to ashes / Harold Pinter. — 1st American ed.
p. cm.
ISBN 0-8021-3510-2
I. Title.
PR6066.I53A9 1997
822'.914—dc21 97-1598

FIRST AMERICAN EDITION

Grove Press
841 Broadway
New York, NY 10003

2 4 6 8 9 7 5 3 1

To Antonia

Ashes to Ashes was first presented by the Royal Court Theatre at the Ambassadors Theatre, London, on 12 September 1996. The cast was as follows:

DEVLIN	Stephen Rea
REBECCA	Lindsay Duncan

Director	Harold Pinter
Designer	Eileen Diss
Lighting	Mick Hughes
Costume	Tom Rand
Sound	Tom Lishman

CHARACTERS

DEVIN
REBECCA

Both in their forties

Time: Now

A house in the country.

Ground floor room. A large window.
Garden beyond.

Two armchairs. Two lamps.

Early evening. Summer.

The room darkens during the course of the play.
The lamplight intensifies.

By the end of the play the room and the garden beyond are only dimly defined.
The lamplight has become very bright but does not illumine the room.

Delvin standing with drink. Rebecca sitting.

Silence.

REBECCA

Well . . . for example . . . he would stand over me and clench his fist. And then he'd put his other hand on my neck and grip it and bring my head towards him. His fist . . . grazed my mouth. And he'd say, 'Kiss my fist.'

DEVLIN

And did you?

REBECCA

Oh yes. I kissed his fist. The knuckles. And then he'd open his hand and give me the palm of his hand . . . to kiss . . . which I kissed.

Pause.

And then I would speak.

DEVLIN

What did you say? You said what? What did you say?

Pause.

REBECCA

I said, 'Put your hand round my throat.' I murmured

it through his hand, as I was kissing it, but he heard my voice, he heard it through his hand, he felt my voice in his hand, he heard it there.

Silence.

DEVLIN

And did he? Did he put his hand round your throat?

REBECCA

Oh yes. He did. He did. And he held it there, very gently, very gently, so gently. He adored me, you see.

DEVLIN

He adored you?

Pause.

What do you mean, he adored you? What do you mean?

Pause.

Are you saying he put no pressure on your throat? Is that what you're saying?

REBECCA

No.

DEVLIN

What then? What are you saying?

REBECCA

He put a little . . . pressure . . . on my throat, yes. So that my head started to go back, gently but truly.

DEVLIN

And your body? Where did your body go?

REBECCA

My body went back, slowly but truly.

DEVLIN

So your legs were opening?

REBECCA

Yes.

Pause.

DEVLIN

Your legs were opening?

REBECCA

Yes.

Silence.

DEVLIN

Do you feel you're being hypnotised?

REBECCA

When?

DEVLIN

Now.

REBECCA

No.

DEVLIN

Really?

REBECCA

No.

DEVLIN

Why not?

REBECCA

Who by?

DEVLIN

By me.

REBECCA

You?

DEVLIN

What do you think?

REBECCA

I think you're a fuckpig.

DEVLIN

Me a fuckpig? Me! You must be joking.

Rebecca smiles.

REBECCA

Me joking? You must be joking.

Pause.

DEVLIN

You understand why I'm asking you these questions. Don't you? Put yourself in my place. I'm compelled to ask you questions. There are so many things I don't know. I know nothing . . . about any of this. Nothing. I'm in the dark. I need light. Or do you think my questions are illegitimate?

Pause.

REBECCA

What questions?

Pause.

DEVLIN

Look. It would mean a great deal to me if you could define him more clearly.

REBECCA

Define him? What do you mean, define him?

DEVLIN

Physically. I mean, what did he actually look like? If you see what I mean? Length, breadth . . . that sort of thing. Height, width. I mean, quite apart from his . . . disposition, whatever that may have been . . . or his character . . . or his spiritual . . . standing . . . I just want, well, I need . . . to have a clearer idea of him . . . well, not a clearer idea . . . just an idea, in fact . . . because I have absolutely no idea . . . as things stand . . . of what he looked like.
I mean, what did he *look like?* Can't you give him a shape for me, a concrete shape? I want a concrete image of him, you see . . . an image I can carry about with me. I mean, all you can talk of are his hands, one hand over your face, the other on the back of your neck, then the first one on your throat. There must be more to him than hands. What about eyes? Did he have any eyes?

REBECCA

What colour?

Pause.

DEVLIN

That's precisely the question I'm asking you . . . my darling.

REBECCA

How odd to be called darling. No one has ever called me darling. Apart from my lover.

DEVLIN

I don't believe it.

REBECCA

You don't believe what?

DEVLIN

I don't believe he ever called you darling.

Pause.

Do you think my use of the word is illegitimate?

REBECCA

What word?

DEVLIN

Darling.

REBECCA

Oh yes, you called me darling. How funny.

DEVLIN

Funny? Why?

REBECCA

Well, how can you possibly call me darling? I'm not your darling.

DEVLIN

Yes you are.

REBECCA

Well I don't want to be your darling. It's the last thing I want to be. I'm nobody's darling.

DEVLIN

That's a song.

REBECCA

What?

DEVLIN

'I'm nobody's baby now'.

REBECCA

It's '*You're* nobody's baby now'. But anyway, I didn't use the word baby.

Pause.

I can't tell you what he looked like.

DEVLIN

Have you forgotten?

REBECCA

No. I haven't forgotten. But that's not the point. Anyway, he went away years ago.

DEVLIN

Went away? Where did he go?

REBECCA

His job took him away. He had a job.

DEVLIN

What was it?

REBECCA

What?

DEVLIN

What kind of job was it? What job?

REBECCA

I think it had something to do with a travel agency. I think he was some kind of courier. No. No, he wasn't. That was only a part-time job. I mean that was only part of the job in the agency. He was quite high up, you see. He had a lot of responsibilities.

Pause.

DEVLIN

What sort of agency?

REBECCA

A travel agency.

DEVLIN

What sort of travel agency?

REBECCA

He was a guide, you see. A guide.

DEVLIN

A tourist guide?

Pause.

REBECCA

Did I ever tell you about that place . . . about the time he took me to that place?

DEVLIN

What place?

REBECCA

I'm sure I told you.

DEVLIN

No. You never told me.

REBECCA

How funny. I could swear I had. Told you.

DEVLIN

You haven't told me anything. You've never spoken about him before. You haven't told me anything.

Pause.

What place?

REBECCA

Oh, it was a kind of factory, I suppose.

DEVLIN

What do you mean, a kind of factory? Was it a factory or wasn't it? And if it was a factory, what kind of factory was it?

REBECCA

Well, they were making things — just like any other factory. But it wasn't the usual kind of factory.

DEVLIN

Why not?

REBECCA

They were all wearing caps . . . the workpeople . . . soft caps . . . and they took them off when he came in, leading me, when he led me down the alleys between the rows of workpeople.

DEVLIN

They took their caps off? You mean they doffed them?

REBECCA

Yes.

DEVLIN

Why did they do that?

REBECCA

He told me afterwards it was because they had such great respect for him.

DEVLIN

Why?

REBECCA

Because he ran a really tight ship, he said. They had total faith in him. They respected his . . . purity, his . . . conviction. They would follow him over a cliff and into the sea, if he asked them, he said. And sing in a chorus, as long as he led them. They were in fact very musical, he said.

DEVLIN

What did they make of you?

REBECCA

Me? Oh, they were sweet. I smiled at them. And immediately every single one of them smiled back.

Pause.

The only thing was — the place was so damp. It was exceedingly damp.

DEVLIN

And they weren't dressed for the weather?

REBECCA

No.

Pause.

DEVLIN

I thought you said he worked for a travel agency?

REBECCA

And there was one other thing. I wanted to go to the bathroom. But I simply couldn't find it. I looked everywhere. I'm sure they had one. But I never found out where it was.

Pause.

He did work for a travel agency. He was a guide. He used to go to the local railway station and walk down the platform and tear all the babies from the arms of their screaming mothers.

Pause.

DEVLIN

Did he?

Silence.

REBECCA

By the way, I'm terribly upset.

DEVLIN

Are you? Why?

REBECCA

Well, it's about that police siren we heard a couple of minutes ago.

DEVLIN

What police siren?

REBECCA

Didn't you hear it? You must have heard it. Just a couple of minutes ago.

DEVLIN

What about it?

REBECCA

Well, I'm just terribly upset.

Pause.

I'm just incredibly upset.

Pause.

Don't you want to know why? Well, I'm going to tell you anyway. If I can't tell you who can I tell? Well, I'll tell you anyway. It just hit me so hard. You see . . . as the siren faded away in my ears I knew it was becoming louder and louder for somebody else.

DEVLIN

You mean that it's always being heard by somebody, somewhere? Is that what you're saying?

REBECCA

Yes. Always. Forever.

DEVLIN

Does that make you feel secure?

REBECCA

No! It makes me feel insecure! Terribly insecure.

DEVLIN

Why?

REBECCA

I hate it fading away. I hate it echoing away. I hate it leaving me. I hate losing it. I hate somebody else possessing it. I want it to be mine, all the time. It's such a beautiful sound. Don't you think?

DEVLIN

Don't worry, there'll always be another one. There's one on its way to you now. Believe me. You'll hear it again soon. Any minute.

REBECCA

Will I?

DEVLIN

Sure. They're very busy people, the police. There's so much for them to do. They've got so much to take care of, to keep their eye on. They keep getting signals, mostly in code. There isn't one minute of the day when they're not charging around one corner or another in the world, in their police cars, ringing their sirens. So you can take comfort from that, at least. Can't you? You'll never be lonely again. You'll never be without a police siren. I promise you.

Pause.

Listen. This chap you were just talking about . . . I mean this chap you and I have been talking about . . . in a manner of speaking . . . when exactly did you meet him? I mean when did all this happen exactly? I haven't . . . how can I put this . . . quite got it into focus. Was it before you knew me or after you knew me? That's a question of some importance. I'm sure you'll appreciate that.

REBECCA

By the way, there's something I've been dying to tell you.

DEVLIN

What?

REBECCA

It was when I was writing a note, a few notes for the

laundry. Well . . . to put it bluntly . . . a laundry list. Well, I put my pen on that little coffee table and it rolled off.

DEVLIN

No?

REBECCA

It rolled right off, onto the carpet. In front of my eyes.

DEVLIN

Good God.

REBECCA

This pen, this perfectly innocent pen.

DEVLIN

You can't know it was innocent.

REBECCA

Why not?

DEVLIN

Because you don't know where it had been. You don't know how many other hands have held it, how many other hands have written with it, what other people have been doing with it. You know nothing of its history. You know nothing of its parents' history.

REBECCA

A pen has no parents.

Pause.

DEVLIN

You can't sit there and say things like that.

REBECCA

I can sit here.

DEVLIN

You can't sit there and say things like that.

REBECCA

You don't believe I'm entitled to sit here? You don't think I'm entitled to sit in this chair, in the place where I live?

DEVLIN

I'm saying that you're not entitled to sit in that chair or in or on any other chair and say things like that and it doesn't matter whether you live here or not.

REBECCA

I'm not entitled to say things like what?

DEVLIN

That that pen was innocent.

REBECCA

You think it was guilty?

Silence.

DEVLIN

I'm letting you off the hook. Have you noticed? I'm letting you slip. Or perhaps it's me who's slipping. It's dangerous. Do you notice? I'm in a quicksand.

REBECCA

Like God.

DEVLIN

God? God? You think God is sinking into a quicksand? That's what I would call a truly disgusting perception. If it can be dignified by the word perception. Be careful how you talk about God. He's the only God we have. If you let him go he won't come back. He won't even look back over his shoulder. And then what will you do? You know what it'll be like, such a vacuum? It'll be like England playing Brazil at Wembley and not a soul in the stadium. Can you imagine? Playing both halves to a totally empty house. The game of the century. Absolute silence. Not a soul watching. Absolute silence. Apart from the referee's whistle and a fair bit of fucking and blinding. If you turn away from God it means that the great and noble game of soccer will fall into permanent oblivion. No score for extra time after extra time after extra time, no score for time

everlasting, for time without end. Absence. Stalemate. Paralysis. A world without a winner.

Pause.

I hope you get the picture.

Pause.

Now let me say this. A little while ago you made . . . shall we say . . . you made a somewhat oblique reference to your bloke . . . your lover? . . . and babies and mothers, etc. And platforms. I inferred from this that you were talking about some kind of atrocity. Now let me ask you this. What authority do you think you yourself possess which would give you the right to discuss such an atrocity?

REBECCA

I have no such authority. Nothing has ever happened to me. Nothing has ever happened to any of my friends. I have never suffered. Nor have my friends.

DEVLIN

Good.

Pause.

Shall we talk more intimately? Let's talk about more intimate things, let's talk about something more personal, about something within your own

immediate experience. I mean, for example, when the hairdresser takes your head in his hands and starts to wash your hair very gently and to massage your scalp, when he does that, when your eyes are closed and he does that, he has your entire trust, doesn't he? It's not just your head which is in his hands, is it, it's your life, it's your spiritual . . . welfare.

Pause.

So you see what I wanted to know was this . . . when your lover had his hand on your throat, did he remind you of your hairdresser?

Pause.

I'm talking about your lover. The man who tried to murder you.

REBECCA

Murder me?

DEVLIN

Do you to death.

REBECCA

No, no. He didn't try to murder me. He didn't want to murder me.

DEVLIN

He suffocated you and strangled you. As near as

makes no difference. According to your account. Didn't he?

REBECCA

No, no. He felt compassion for me. He adored me.

Pause.

DEVLIN

Did he have a name, this chap? Was he a foreigner? And where was I at the time? What do you want me to understand? Were you unfaithful to me? Why didn't you confide in me? Why didn't you confess? You would have felt so much better. Honestly. You could have treated me like a priest. You could have put me on my mettle. I've always wanted to be put on my mettle. It used to be one of my lifetime ambitions. Now I've missed my big chance. Unless all this happened before I met you. In which case you have no obligation to tell me anything. Your past is not my business. I wouldn't dream of telling you about my past. Not that I had one. When you lead a life of scholarship you can't be bothered with the humorous realities, you know, tits, that kind of thing. Your mind is on other things, have you got an attentive landlady, can she come up with bacon and eggs after eleven o'clock at night, is the bed warm, does the sun rise in the right direction, is the soup cold? Only once in a blue moon do you wobble the chambermaid's bottom, on the assumption there is one — chambermaid not bottom —

but of course none of this applies when you have a wife. When you have a wife you let thought, ideas and reflection take their course. Which means you never let the best man win. Fuck the best man, that's always been my motto. It's the man who ducks his head and moves on through no matter what wind or weather who gets there in the end. A man with guts and application.

Pause.

A man who doesn't give a shit.
A man with a rigid sense of duty.

Pause.

There's no contradiction between those last two statements. Believe me.

Pause.

Do you follow the drift of my argument?

REBECCA

Oh yes, there's something I've forgotten to tell you. It was funny. I looked out of the garden window, out of the window into the garden, in the middle of summer, in that house in Dorset, do you remember? Oh no, you weren't there. I don't think anyone else was there. No. I was all by myself. I was alone. I was looking out of the window and I saw a whole crowd

of people walking through the woods, on their way to the sea, in the direction of the sea. They seemed to be very cold, they were wearing coats, although it was such a beautiful day. A beautiful, warm, Dorset day. They were carrying bags. There were . . . guides . . . ushering them, guiding them along. They walked through the woods and I could see them in the distance walking across the cliff and down to the sea. Then I lost sight of them. I was really quite curious so I went upstairs to the highest window in the house and I looked way over the top of the treetops and I could see down to the beach. The guides . . . were ushering all these people across the beach. It was such a lovely day. It was so still and the sun was shining. And I saw all these people walk into the sea. The tide covered them slowly. Their bags bobbed about in the waves.

DEVLIN

When was that? When did you live in Dorset? I've never lived in Dorset.

Pause.

REBECCA

Oh by the way somebody told me the other day that there's a condition known as mental elephantiasis.

DEVLIN

What do you mean, 'somebody told you'? What do you mean, 'the other day'? What are you talking about?

REBECCA

This mental elephantiasis means that when you spill an ounce of gravy, for example, it immediately expands and becomes a vast sea of gravy. It becomes a sea of gravy which surrounds you on all sides and you suffocate in a voluminous sea of gravy. It's terrible. But it's all your own fault. You brought it upon yourself. You are not the *victim* of it, you are the *cause* of it. Because it was you who spilt the gravy in the first place, it was you who handed over the bundle.

Pause.

DEVLIN

The what?

REBECCA

The bundle.

Pause.

DEVLIN

So what's the question? Are you prepared to drown in your own gravy? Or are you prepared to die for your country? Look. What do you say, sweetheart? Why don't we go out and drive into town and take in a movie?

REBECCA

That's funny, somewhere in a dream . . . a long time ago . . . I heard someone calling me sweetheart.

Pause.

I looked up. I'd been dreaming. I don't know whether I looked up in the dream or as I opened my eyes. But in this dream a voice was calling. That I'm certain of. This voice was calling me. It was calling me sweetheart.

Pause.

Yes.

Pause.

I walked out into the frozen city. Even the mud was frozen. And the snow was a funny colour. It wasn't white. Well, it was white but there were other colours in it. It was as if there were veins running through it. And it wasn't smooth, as snow is, as snow should be. It was bumpy. And when I got to the railway station I saw the train. Other people were there.

Pause.

And my best friend, the man I had given my heart to, the man I knew was the man for me the moment we met, my dear, my most precious companion, I watched him walk down the platform and tear all the babies from the arms of their screaming mothers.

Silence.

DEVLIN

Did you see Kim and the kids?

She looks at him.

You were going to see Kim and the kids today.

She stares at him.

Your sister Kim and the kids.

REBECCA

Oh, Kim! And the kids, yes. Yes. Yes, of course I saw them. I had tea with them. Didn't I tell you?

DEVLIN

No.

REBECCA

Of course I saw them.

Pause.

DEVLIN

How were they?

REBECCA

Ben's talking.

DEVLIN

Really? What's he saying?

REBECCA

Oh, things like 'My name is Ben'. Things like that. And 'Mummy's name is Mummy'. Things like that.

DEVLIN

What about Betsy?

REBECCA

She's crawling.

DEVLIN

No, really?

REBECCA

I think she'll be walking before we know where we are. Honestly.

DEVLIN

Probably talking too. Saying things like 'My name is Betsy'.

REBECCA

Yes, of course I saw them. I had tea with them. But oh . . . my poor sister . . . she doesn't know what to do.

DEVLIN

What do you mean?

REBECCA

Well, he wants to come back . . . you know. . . he keeps phoning and asking her to take him back. He says he can't bear it, he says he's given the other one up, he says he's living quite alone, he's given the other one up.

DEVLIN

Has he?

REBECCA

He says he has. He says he misses the kids.

Pause.

DEVLIN

Does he miss his wife?

REBECCA

He says he's given the other one up. He says it was never serious, you know, it was only sex.

DEVLIN

Ah.

Pause.

And Kim?

Pause.

And Kim?

REBECCA

She'll never have him back. Never. She says she'll never share a bed with him again. Never. Ever.

DEVLIN

Why not?

REBECCA

Never ever.

DEVLIN

But why not?

REBECCA

Of course I saw Kim and the kids. I had tea with them. Why did you ask? Did you think I didn't see them?

DEVLIN

No. I didn't know. It's just that you said you were going to have tea with them.

REBECCA

Well, I did have tea with them! Why shouldn't I? She's my sister.

Pause.

Guess where I went after tea? To the cinema. I saw a film.

DEVLIN

Oh? What?

REBECCA

A comedy.

DEVLIN

Uh-huh? Was it funny? Did you laugh?

REBECCA

Other people laughed. Other members of the audience. It was funny.

DEVLIN

But you didn't laugh?

REBECCA

Other people did. It was a comedy. There was a girl . . . you know . . . and a man. They were having lunch in a smart New York restaurant. He made her smile.

DEVLIN

How?

REBECCA

Well . . . he told her jokes.

DEVLIN

Oh, I see.

REBECCA

And then in the next scene he took her on an expedition to the desert, in a caravan. She'd never lived in a desert before, you see. She had to learn how to do it.

Pause.

DEVLIN

Sounds very funny.

REBECCA

But there was a man sitting in front of me, to my right. He was absolutely still throughout the whole film. He never moved, he was rigid, like a body with rigor mortis, he never laughed once, he just sat like a corpse. I moved far away from him, I moved as far away from him as I possibly could.

Silence.

DEVLIN

Now look, let's start again. We live here. You don't live . . . in Dorset . . . or *anywhere else.* You live here with me. This is our house. You have a very nice sister. She lives close to you. She has two lovely kids. You're their aunt. You like that.

Pause.

You have a wonderful garden. You love your garden. You created it all by yourself. You have truly green fingers. You also have beautiful fingers.

Pause.

Did you hear what I said? I've just paid you a compliment. In fact I've just paid you a number of compliments. Let's start again.

REBECCA

I don't think we can start again. We started . . . a long time ago. We started. We can't start *again*. We can end again.

DEVLIN

But we've never ended.

REBECCA

Oh, we have. Again and again and again. And we can end again. And again and again. And again.

DEVLIN

Aren't you misusing the word 'end'? End means end. You can't end 'again'. You can only end once.

REBECCA

No. You can end once and then you can end again.

Silence.

(*singing softly*) 'Ashes to ashes' —

DEVLIN

'And dust to dust' —

REBECCA

'If the women don't get you' —

DEVLIN

'The liquor must.'

Pause.

I always knew you loved me.

REBECCA

Why?

DEVLIN

Because we like the same tunes.

Silence.

Listen.

Pause.

Why have you never told me about this lover of yours before this? I have the right to be very angry

indeed. Do you realise that? I have the right to be very angry indeed. Do you understand that?

Silence.

REBECCA

Oh by the way there's something I meant to tell you. I was standing in a room at the top of a very tall building in the middle of town. The sky was full of stars. I was about to close the curtains but I stayed at the window for a time looking up at the stars. Then I looked down. I saw an old man and a little boy walking down the street. They were both dragging suitcases. The little boy's suitcase was bigger than he was. It was a very bright night. Because of the stars. The old man and the little boy were walking down the street. They were holding each other's free hand. I wondered where they were going. Anyway, I was about to close the curtains but then I suddenly saw a woman following them, carrying a baby in her arms.

Pause.

Did I tell you the street was icy? It was icy. So she had to tread very carefully. Over the bumps. The stars were out. She followed the man and the boy until they turned the corner and were gone.

Pause.

She stood still. She kissed her baby. The baby was a girl.

Pause.

She kissed her.

Pause.

She listened to the baby's heartbeat. The baby's heart was beating.

The light in the room has darkened. The lamps are very bright.

Rebecca sits very still.

The baby was breathing.

Pause.

I held her to me. She was breathing. Her heart was beating.

Devlin goes to her. He stands over her and looks down at her.
He clenches his fist and holds it in front of her face. He puts his left hand behind her neck and grips it. He brings her head towards his fist. His fist touches her mouth.

DEVLIN

Kiss my fist.

She does not move.

He opens his hand and places the palm of his hand on her mouth.

She does not move.

DEVLIN

Speak. Say it. Say 'Put your hand round my throat.'

She does not speak.

Ask me to put my hand round your throat.

She does not speak or move.

He puts his hand on her throat. He presses gently. Her head goes back.

They are still.

She speaks. There is an echo. His grip loosens.

REBECCA

They took us to the trains

ECHO

the trains

He takes his hand from her throat.

REBECCA

They were taking the babies away

ECHO

the babies away

Pause.

REBECCA

I took my baby and wrapped it in my shawl

ECHO

my shawl

REBECCA

And I made it into a bundle

ECHO

a bundle

REBECCA

And I held it under my left arm

ECHO

my left arm

Pause.

REBECCA

And I went through with my baby

ECHO

my baby

Pause.

REBECCA

But the baby cried out

ECHO

cried out

REBECCA

And the man called me back

ECHO

called me back

REBECCA

And he said what do you have there

ECHO

have there

REBECCA

He stretched out his hand for the bundle

ECHO

for the bundle

REBECCA

And I gave him the bundle

ECHO

the bundle

REBECCA

And that's the last time I held the bundle

ECHO

the bundle

Silence.

REBECCA

And we got on the train

ECHO

the train

REBECCA

And we arrived at this place

ECHO

this place

REBECCA

And I met a woman I knew

ECHO

I knew

REBECCA
And she said what happened to your baby

ECHO
your baby

REBECCA
Where is your baby

ECHO
your baby

REBECCA
And I said what baby

ECHO
what baby

REBECCA
I don't have a baby

ECHO
a baby

REBECCA
I don't know of any baby

ECHO
of any baby

Pause.

REBECCA

I don't know of any baby

Long silence.

BLACKOUT